8|18

WHITE AND BLACK HAT HACKERS

Cryptography: Code Making and Code Breaking

WHITE AND BLACK HAT HACKERS

Jason Porterfield

New York

Published in 2017 by The Rosen Publishing Group, Inc.
29 East 21st Street, New York, NY 10010

First Edition

Library of Congress Cataloging-in-Publication Data

Names: Porterfield, Jason, author.
Title: White and black hat hackers / Jason Porterfield.
Description: First edition. | New York : Rosen Publishing, 2017. | Series: Cryptography : code making and code breaking | Includes bibliographical references and index.
Identifiers: LCCN 2016017849 | ISBN 9781508173144 (library bound)
Subjects: LCSH: Penetration testing (Computer security)—Juvenile literature. | Computer security—Juvenile literature. | Computer crimes—Juvenile literature. | Computer crimes—Prevention—Juvenile literature.
Classification: LCC TK5105.59 .P66 2017 | DDC 005.8—dc23
LC record available at https://lccn.loc.gov/2016017849

Manufactured in China

CONTENTS

INTRODUCTION

In many ways, computers are wonderful tools. They store huge amounts of information, control important processes, and keep systems running smoothly. Computers can solve problems and find solutions far faster than humans, and they can be used to help predict outcomes of everything from global warming to baseball games. Specialized computers control transportation systems, computer networks, and even financial transactions.

Famed hacker Barnaby Jack once worked as a white hat hacker, testing the security of medical devices such as insulin pumps for technical weaknesses.

Computers are also tempting targets for curious people and criminals. Hackers are individuals who gain access to computers or networks without official permission. They may be computer enthusiasts who want to find out how security systems work, specialists trying to strengthen the network, thieves intent on causing damage, or activists trying to prove a point.

Black hat hackers are those who want to steal information or cause damage. The name comes from old Westerns—the movies, dramas, or novels in which bad guys such as bank robbers or cattle rustlers wear black hats, and the sheriff and other cowboy heroes wear white hats.

All hackers have a deep knowledge of computers and networks. They are curious about the way systems are set up and how programs are coded. However, white hat hackers are interested in building systems and making them stronger, while black hats want to tear them apart. They exploit security flaws to steal information and cause chaos. They tamper with systems and write viruses designed to shut networks down. Gray hats fall somewhere in between, as they access computers without permission but rarely do so with criminal intent.

Where black hat hackers want to break into systems, white hat hackers are concerned with making data more secure. They are often employed to help companies expose vulnerabilities in their security systems and make them more secure. Some of these ethical hackers were once black hat hackers who were interested in violating or compromising security, often to steal money or information.

Legally, the difference between white hat and black hat hackers is simple: white hat hackers have been given permission to break into systems to perform a job. Cracking into a network without permission—even if one's intentions are good—is still considered illegal and falls into the shady area of gray hat hacking.

Hacking as a hobby and pastime blossomed during the 1980s. Personal computers were becoming more common in businesses and homes. Criminals were also becoming aware that valuable data was being stored on computers and that they could steal money, software, and secrets by hacking into those computers. The introduction of the World Wide Web in the 1990s opened up greater possibilities for theft and mischief. Today, computers and the internet play a huge role in people's lives, from providing vital services to delivering entertainment. It is more important than ever for white hat hackers to keep the black hats at bay.

CHAPTER 1

HACKING'S EARLY DAYS

Hacking dates back to the late 1800s, when people would gain unauthorized access to early telephone networks and disrupt telegraph messages. Even some of the earliest radio broadcasts were intercepted by people other than their intended recipients. During the 1960s, hackers were people who could find shortcuts within the huge mainframe computers in use at the time and make the machines perform unexpected tasks. Today, hackers try to access computers through networks that span the globe.

TRAIN SETS TO MAINFRAMES

The practice of hacking can be traced back to the earliest telegraph networks, which were first developed in the 1840s and could be used to send messages over long distances in a matter of minutes. People sometimes tapped telegraph lines to get the messages. This practice became an easy way for spies to steal information about companies, governments, and armies. People eventually started using secret codes so that important messages could remain confidential.

Early experiments in radio broadcasts were also plagued by people listening in without permission. In 1895, Italian inventor and radio pioneer Guglielmo Marconi invented the first practical means of sending telegraph

Guglielmo Marconi's wireless devices paved the way for modern radio and cell phones. However, the messages sent using his radio transmitters were not as secure as he advertised.

messages using radio waves. During a public demonstration held in London, England, in 1903, a magician and inventor named John Nevil Maskelyne intercepted Marconi's radio frequencies and delivered an insulting message to the audience. The incident embarrassed Marconi and proved his technology was not as secure as he claimed.

Punch-card computers were also vulnerable to hackers, even though they were not connected to any networks. During World War II, a French punch-card computer expert and government official named René Carmille and several others altered equipment to disrupt the pro-Nazi government's efforts to track Jewish citizens. Their sabotage efforts went undetected from 1940 to 1944 and likely saved thousands of lives.

THE ORIGINS OF HACKER CULTURE

The word "hacking" was first associated with technology through the experiments of a club at the Massachusetts Institute of Technology (MIT). The Tech Model Railroad Club's members modified electric train sets to make them faster, a process they called "hacking." Some of the club's members were also interested in computers and in finding new ways to make them work. The computers that were available at the time were massive machines, each big enough to fill a room. These mainframes were accessible only on-site. They were also very expensive and generally owned by only governments, schools, and large companies. In many cases, access to the machines was limited to just a few well-trained specialists. Several members of the club impressed the manager of the MIT Artificial Intelligence Lab enough that he gave them access to the lab's machines. They began calling themselves the Signal and Power Committee and took an interest in creating programming tools.

Early computers required enormous amounts of space because they relied on arrays of vacuum tubes and transistors. MIT's hackers were always working to improve the computers' speed and functionality.

Computer hacking spread quickly after the US Department of Defense developed the first large, high-speed computer network in 1969. The Advanced Research Projects Agency Network (ARPANET) was first built as an experiment in digital communication and was based on a computer science principle called packet switching. In packet switching, software breaks data down into small blocks called packets, which are sent out over wires or via satellite. When the packets arrive, software puts them together so that the data can be seen as intended.

ARPANET connected scientists and researchers at labs and universities in a new way, allowing them to communicate instantly and share ideas. The network eventually grew to include two hundred locations and formed an early version of the internet. Four universities—MIT, Stanford in California, Carnegie-Mellon in Pennsylvania, and the University of California in Los Angeles—were also connected to ARPANET. Hacker groups similar to the one at MIT formed at those other universities. Connected through ARPANET, they were able to share ideas. They traded software and developed their own slang, developing a new hacker subculture. These early hackers, most of whom were driven by their curiosity and their interest in improving computers, can be classified as white hat hackers.

ARPANET was a project of the United States military, and the government's Central Intelligence Agency (CIA) was heavily involved. The military wanted a computer network that would allow secure and instant communication. It was also important for some files shared over the network to be accessible by only certain people. After ARPANET was developed, the US Department of Defense encouraged hackers to try to break into its computer systems to find any weak points.

The white hat hackers who were able to get around ARPANET's security provided valuable feedback on how to improve security. Early on, the network didn't require users to log in with passwords. Password protection was added to sensitive files to serve as an initial layer of defense. Digital encryption systems were also invented to make it harder to crack into password-protected files.

Cryptography is the practice and process of turning readable text into something that cannot be read. A device called a cipher is used to turn the message into nonsense and then to return it to readable form. People have used cryptography to send private or secret messages for thousands of years. Cryptography was used in the 1940s and 1950s to make early digital, programmable computers secure. It became more and more complex throughout the twentieth century. Mathematical algorithms were developed to make encryption harder to break.

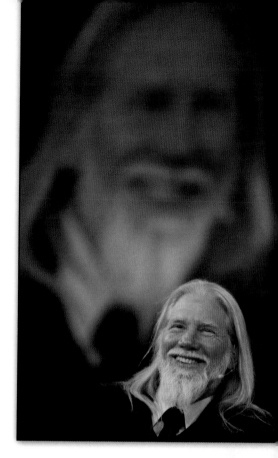

Whitfield Diffie revolutionized digital security through the concept of public-key cryptography. He went on to become a vocal advocate for digital privacy.

In 1976, cryptographers Whitfield Diffie and Martin Hellman published an academic paper titled "New Directions in Cryptography." They established a system of encryption called "key cryptography," which uses numerical codes and algorithms to protect data. Today, key encryption is widely used to protect email messages, credit card information, corporate documents, and other valuable data from hackers.

PHONE PHREAKING

In 1957, a blind seven-year-old boy named Joe Engressia accidentally discovered that he could make long-distance telephone calls by whistling a certain tone into the phone's receiver. Little did Engressia know that a subculture of people called "phreakers" worked to understand the phone systems and illegally take advantage of them. They experimented with whistles, electrical pulses, and homemade "blue box" electrical devices that allowed them to dial into phone systems. A colorful subculture rose out of phreaking, one that resembled and sometimes crossed over with that of the early hackers. Technology upgrades eventually ended most forms of phreaking in the 1980s.

HACKING IN THE SHADOWS

In the years that followed ARPANET's creation, universities, research facilities, and some private companies developed their own internal networks. These local area networks (LANs) connected one computer located within a department with all of the other computers there, so that users could share information electronically. Each LAN could connect with other LANs, creating a network of many computers and users. The contributions of white hat hackers helped make these networks possible.

Not every hacker had good intentions. The increasing use of computers for sharing information motivated black hat hackers to target networks. The first malicious (malware) programs, commonly known as viruses and worms, started innocently. However, they evolved into problems that affected computer users worldwide and that would be used by black hat hackers for decades to come.

Viruses are pieces of computer code that are able to copy themselves over and over. They are loaded onto computers without the user's knowledge and run against the user's wishes, making undesired changes to the way the computer runs. Some viruses are relatively harmless, but others can do serious damage by corrupting software and erasing memory.

In 1982, a teenager named Rich Skrenta wrote a virus program called Elk Cloner as a prank. Skrenta designed Elk Cloner to hop from corrupted disc to uncorrupted disc. The virus was spread quickly to other computers by users trading infected discs. It became the first virus to spread in the "wild." Viruses have since become much more widespread, harming computers around the world.

Worms are malware programs that can copy themselves and infect multiple computers. Unlike viruses, they don't need to attach themselves to other programs to spread. The first worm was introduced by the Xerox Palo Alto Research Center in 1982. It was a legitimate program designed to perform network maintenance tasks, though its developers noted the difficulty of

Rich Skrenta was a teenager when he used this Apple II Plus to create the Elk Cloner virus. Unlike later viruses, Elk Cloner was originally intended as a joke.

controlling the worm's ability to make new copies of itself.

In 1988, Cornell University student Robert Tappan Morris designed a worm and released it over the internet. It became known as the Morris Worm and infected two thousand computers within fifteen hours, attracting national attention. In 1989, black hat hackers released the first true malware worm, called the Internet Worm, which spread among UNIX systems connected through the internet and caused widespread denials of service. Like viruses, worms remain serious threats to computer security, giving black hat hackers the ability to shut down entire networks and cause significant damage to important data.

During the 1980s, criminals began using computers to commit acts of fraud. Several early black hat hackers became infamous for their direct intrusions against network security. Rather than hacking into networks out of curiosity or to help solve security problems, they sought to steal money or information. Data breaches and the spread of worms and viruses led to the US Congress passing the Computer Fraud and Abuse Act in 1986. The federal law has been amended several times to keep up with technological advances.

Vladimir Levin was a Russian working out of London, England, who led a large international crime ring. In 1995, he accessed Citibank accounts using stolen passwords and other data and illegally transferred $3.7 million. Levin was eventually captured by the Federal Bureau of Investigation (FBI). In 1998, he was sentenced to three years in prison.

During the 1980s, German citizen Markus Hess hacked into US military computers through a university network on behalf of the Soviet Union. A systems administrator discovered the breach in 1986. The FBI eventually caught him by inventing a phony military project and then tracing him as he accessed it. Hess was captured in Germany and convicted of espionage, receiving a suspended sentence. In all, the Soviet Union paid him just $54,000 for his hacking.

WORLD WIDE WEB REVOLUTION

The growth of the World Wide Web in the late 1990s brought more people online. The web gave people the means to communicate with others and access information from their own computers. The World Wide Web today carries an incredible flow of information. People use it in ways that would have been unimaginable when it was first developed. The web now influences how people learn their way around towns, how they do research, and even how they find out the date and temperature.

Today, more information than ever before is stored on computers and is being transmitted through the internet. This information includes personal particulars such as financial and medical records, government data, including records and classified communications, and information belonging to groups and companies. That data is typically stored on secured servers. Networks are designed to deny unauthorized access. Security measures such as firewalls and encryption keys protect important information from digital intruders, but cybercriminals are always looking for ways to get around them.

CHAPTER 2

THE SHADY SIDE OF SECURITY

Hackers have become key figures in the world of information security. However, the use of white hat hackers—particularly former black hat hackers—to seek out vulnerabilities raises the very important question of trust. How can companies and government agencies trust white hat hackers to find ways into their systems and then avoid the temptation of stealing that data and profiting from it? There are no guarantees that they will remain honest. However, money can be a motivating factor. Many white hat hackers are paid very large fees so that they are not tempted to steal data or cause problems. They enter into legal contracts that bind them to honest and ethical behavior. Breaking those contracts could lead to lawsuits and criminal charges.

The famous hackers who work as white hat consultants are often known to the public because they've been caught hacking. They may have been arrested in the past. If they were convicted, they may have been fined, put on probation, or even sent to jail. They would probably face more serious punishment if they were again caught hacking illegally. Faced with that possibility and a desire to put their skills and knowledge to work, they instead become white hat hackers.

Others stay on the white hat side because they follow a strict moral code. Their beliefs prevent them from taking on illegal hacking projects, at least against the companies and organizations that hire them. The same moral code also may lead white hat hackers down a slippery slope and into "hacktivism," which is the practice of hacking the data of groups,

White hat hackers such as Marc Maiffret (left) and Firas Bushnaq of eEye Digital Security apply their skills to finding vulnerabilities for Microsoft and other companies.

companies, individuals, or governments to deliver a message. Some white hat hackers get so caught up in hactivism causes that they will perform unauthorized hacking jobs.

DEVELOPING SECURITY

Early law enforcement methods of catching hackers were usually limited to looking at the phone records and computer logs of suspects. Although early white hats had been present throughout the development of ARPANET, there were few working outside of government or university labs. That situation began changing after the release of several malicious programs in the mid-1980s. The US government created the US

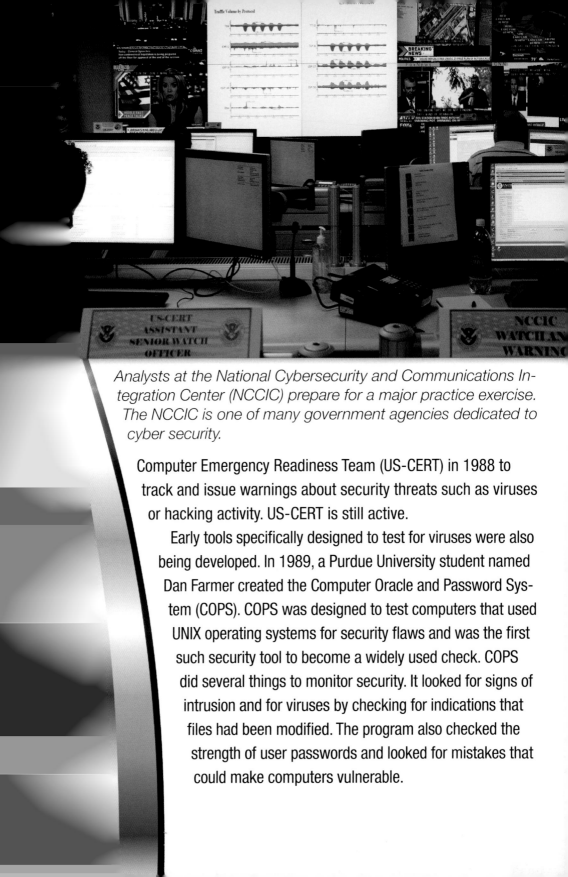

Analysts at the National Cybersecurity and Communications Integration Center (NCCIC) prepare for a major practice exercise. The NCCIC is one of many government agencies dedicated to cyber security.

Computer Emergency Readiness Team (US-CERT) in 1988 to track and issue warnings about security threats such as viruses or hacking activity. US-CERT is still active.

Early tools specifically designed to test for viruses were also being developed. In 1989, a Purdue University student named Dan Farmer created the Computer Oracle and Password System (COPS). COPS was designed to test computers that used UNIX operating systems for security flaws and was the first such security tool to become a widely used check. COPS did several things to monitor security. It looked for signs of intrusion and for viruses by checking for indications that files had been modified. The program also checked the strength of user passwords and looked for mistakes that could make computers vulnerable.

In 1995, Farmer and another programmer named Wietse Venema developed another set of programs called the Security Administrator Tools for Analyzing Networks (SATAN). The SATAN program suite, which was available for free, broke new ground by using many of the most widespread hacker tactics to check for vulnerabilities that could be used to gain access through networks. The programs were controversial because some security professionals believed they would make it easier to hack systems. Hackers sometimes used it to test systems for vulnerabilities before trying to gain access. The US Justice Department even investigated the software's development and threatened to press charges against Farmer's employer, Silicon Graphics.

SATAN co-developer Dan Farmer acknowledged that even though the program suite was created to help strengthen networks, hackers and spies could also use it to probe for weaknesses.

In the years since Dan Farmer developed SATAN, white hat hacking has become standard practice for many businesses. The focus of computer security shifted from one of reacting to threats after the fact to one of trying to anticipate breaches and prevent them. This means updating security systems regularly as new threats emerge.

Since the early 1990s, the most frequently used network security tools have been firewalls and digital certificates. Firewalls prevent hackers from hijacking programs or using them to create back doors to networks or computers. Digital certificates (or digital certification) are issued by trusted vendors and are designed to show that a particular user has permission to access the protected information. They use a numeric key system to authenticate users. If the user's key matches, a certificate is issued to the user's computer, allowing the user to see the protected data. The keys themselves are long algorithms and are designed to be very difficult to crack, though breaches are possible.

REIMAGINING HACKING

Hackers hired to try to break into networks provide a valuable service by demonstrating the effectiveness of the security measures that are already in place. They know the tricks black hat hackers use to gain access. Their clients are often businesses that people trust with their most personal information. Many of the biggest companies in the United States hire white hats to test their security. Banks, insurance companies, and health care providers are among the businesses that hire white hat hackers to check their digital security. Big retailers and service providers such as phone and cable

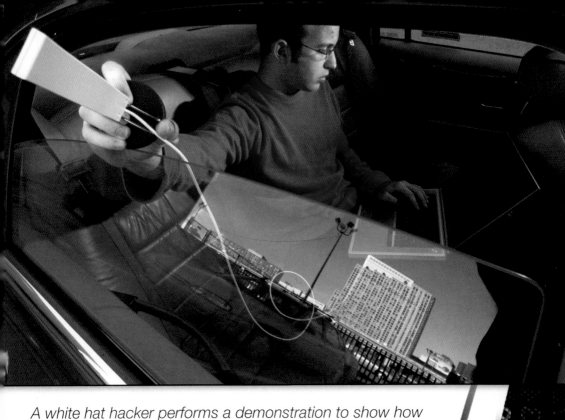

A white hat hacker performs a demonstration to show how easily a wireless network can be penetrated by using a laptop from the back of a taxi.

companies also sometimes hire hackers to gather information about possible flaws in their security.

White hat hackers probe networks for new or unexpected vulnerabilities. This process is called penetration testing. Penetration tests usually start by checking for security problems at the most basic points of entry and then moving inward. Hackers may begin by probing ports, testing known software defects, and examining the patches that have been installed to fix them. They also look for weak points within the company's structure and phish for access to systems. Once the white hat gains access, he or she reports back to the organization's information technology department so that those professionals can fix the problems.

VEHICLE VULNERABILITIES

In 2015, white hat hackers Charlie Miller and Chris Valasek managed to remotely access the controls of a Jeep Cherokee. Working in tandem with a journalist for *Wired* magazine, the hackers accessed the vehicle's controls through its computer system and manipulated the radio, windshield wipers, and air conditioner before disabling the Jeep. Miller and Valasek had hacked vehicles before, but this experiment showed they could do so from ten miles (sixteen kilometers) away. Many functions on recently manufactured vehicles are now automatic and controlled by computers, and hackers could put many lives at risk by accessing them. Vehicle manufacturers are also quick to point out that it would be very difficult for most people to hack into a car's computer.

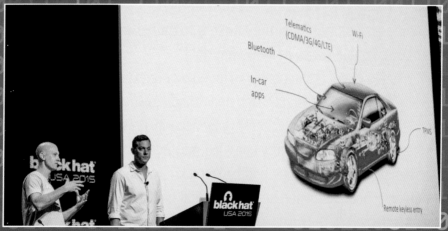

By taking control of an automobile, white hat hackers Charlie Miller (left) and Chris Valasek exposed just how vulnerable many everyday activities such as driving are to hackers.

In a case in which the hacker is testing an entire organization's data security, he or she may engage in shady activity that would be illegal without permission from the people in charge. Often, only a handful of officials within the organization are aware of the test. The hacker's activities might include trying to trick employees into revealing clues that can be used to figure out passwords, leaving flash drives loaded with malicious programs around the office, or sending employees Trojan horse programs as seemingly innocent attachments. These are all tactics that are used by black hat hackers. The results of these efforts might be used by the company or organization to improve its security training.

Large companies and even government agencies might pay white hats thousands of dollars per hour to perform penetration testing against their servers. They want these ethical hackers to find any security holes or vulnerabilities so that they can be repaired before a black hat hacker discovers them.

A white hat hacker ends the intrusion as soon as he or she gets access to the targeted network, rather than gathering the valuable data exposed by the hack. Examining any of the protected data would be a breach of ethics and push the hacker into—at best—gray hat territory. Instead, the hacker prepares a report on the hack, what was involved, what computers or servers were exposed, and how such a breach might be avoided in the future.

The recommendations offered by white hat hackers often start with telling the client to make sure that the most current versions of software programs are being used. Older software is often unsupported by the manufacturer and may be more prone to bugs and weaknesses. Hackers have also had more time to study older programs and may be more likely to find vulnerabilities or figure out new ways to exploit weak points. Businesses may also be encouraged to keep in contact with their vendors, contractors, and other partners and share information about breaches or other suspicious activity.

The internet revolutionized how governments and businesses function. People find themselves relying more and more on the internet and the World Wide Web to get through their daily lives. Work, shopping, studying, banking, and numerous other tasks are handled via computer—or smartphones and tablets. Evolving technology has brought about even greater connectivity. Televisions, video game systems, automobiles, and even some household appliances are now designed with the ability to connect to the internet.

Advances in technology have made smart homes—homes with automated appliances and systems that can be programmed or controlled remotely—more available. Heating and air conditioning, lights, and security features such as locks and cameras can be controlled through applications on the homeowner's smartphone. If alarms, security cameras, and even door locks are all connected through the same network, it could be possible for a black hat hacker to make a person's home vulnerable to burglars or other criminals.

CHAPTER 3

MISCHIEF AND THREATS

Black hat hackers are the polar opposites of white hat hackers. White hat hackers are often motivated by curiosity and the desire to improve security, but black hat hackers tend to be driven by a desire to cause trouble. They are actually the illegal and unethical computer experts that most people think of when they hear the word "hacker."

The term "black hat" was coined by computer programming pioneer and free software advocate Richard Stallman, who wanted to contrast the illegal activities against the playful exploration that marked early hacker culture and the ethics that govern white hat hacking. Ethical or white hat hackers are so reluctant to refer to black hats as "hackers" that they sometimes call them "crackers" because they crack into secure systems to cause trouble.

MOTIVES FOR HACKING

Like their white hat counterparts, black hat hackers have deep knowledge of computers and networks. They are curious about the way systems are set up and how programs are coded. However, white hat hackers are interested in building systems and making them stronger. Black hats want to tear them apart. They exploit security flaws to steal information and cause chaos. They tamper with systems and write viruses designed to shut networks down.

Black hats target victims for various reasons. Some make money through a form of digital ransom. They steal data and threaten to release it unless they are paid. Hackers might ransom sensitive information about a company's customers or clients, or they may steal trade secrets and threaten to make them public.

Individuals are also sometimes the victims of digital ransom attempts. Their personal accounts might be hacked and private information stolen for ransom. Banking information, credit card numbers, or medical records might fall into the category of information that hackers hold hostage. In extreme cases, hackers write malware programs that can lock users out of their own computers unless they meet the hackers' demands.

Other information is stolen to be sold. Certain criminals pay for data taken from certain companies. These digital thefts might benefit individuals, companies, organizations, or even nations by providing them with information they may not have been able to get honestly.

Some black hat hackers are motivated by vendettas. They may feel that a person, a company, or even a government agency has harmed them in some way. They seek their revenge through hacking. Ideology also drives some hackers.

Many governments are actively involved in hacking activities against other countries. In recent years, concentrated online attacks against targets in the United States have been linked to China, while evidence shows that the United States has undertaken its own hacking projects against China.

There are also hackers who simply enjoy the act of breaking into systems. The internet gives them the ability to reach out across hundreds or even thousands of miles through their computers. If they are knowledgeable enough, clever enough, and stealthy enough, they might be able to intrude on a secured system without

The hacker Hector Xavier Monsegur (right), known as Sabu, directed hundreds of cyber attacks against corporations and foreign governments before his arrest in 2011.

being detected. Many hackers—whether black hat, white hat, or gray hat—start out this way, driven by the thrill of intruding on a system without permission. As harmless as their intentions may be, these curious, thrill-seeking hackers are breaking the law through their actions.

BLACK HAT TARGETS

Computers were once massive machines that were used only by specially trained scientists and technicians. Smartphones are more powerful than the first

Romanian authorities transport Marcel Lazar Lehel, known as the hacker Guccifer, to court. He allegedly hacked accounts belonging to important personalities, including former US Secretary of State Colin Powell.

computers. The growth of the World Wide Web led to more innovative ways to use computers. Many people don't think twice about using the internet to pay bills, shop, plan vacations, and watch videos. Unfortunately, the same technology that makes it so easy to do things online also exposes people to the dangers of hacking.

Many black hats hack for personal gain, whether they intend to sell the information or use it themselves to commit fraud. Financial institutions such as banks and lenders have been targeted with attempts to steal account information. The Internal Revenue Service (IRS) is a favorite target because of the many personal details available on tax returns.

GRAY HAT HACKERS

Like black hat hackers, gray hat hackers access computers and systems without permission. Their motives are usually different. Gray hats are usually interested in learning about their targets or even just challenging themselves to access protected information, rather than in creating problems. They don't exploit the vulnerabilities they discover, but they also might choose not to report them.

Gray hat hackers have discovered key vulnerabilities in several high-profile cases. In 2013, a gray hat hacker named Khalil Shreateh tried to notify Facebook of a security flaw that could be used to hack profile pages. The company ignored him, so he revealed it to the public by using it to access the profile page of founder Mark Zuckerberg. The vulnerability was repaired soon after that incident.

Government agencies are frequently targeted by hackers. During the early days of the internet, computer enthusiasts would sometimes try to access a government system because they wanted to challenge themselves. There still are hackers who try to crack into agencies just to see if they have the skill to do it, but the majority of attempts are likely committed by people with other motivations. Some are attempting to steal information or spy on behalf of other nations. Others are driven by greed and are hoping to steal data belonging to citizens.

Transportation services such as railways and airports, vital services such as health care networks, and utilities such as phone companies and electricity providers are increasingly vulnerable. Automated functions can be hacked into and manipulated, potentially causing problems ranging from service outages to dangerous situations.

Internal Revenue Service (IRS) Commissioner John Koskinen testifies before the US Senate in 2015. The IRS has been the victim of several embarrassing cyber security breaches in recent years.

Businesses are often targeted. Trade secrets and inside information about deals or finances tempt hackers who go after large corporations. Small businesses may be hacked for customer data or information about suppliers and clients. Hacking attempts are made against smaller businesses because black hats believe these companies may have weak security.

ONLINE HAZARDS

Individuals are increasingly becoming the victims of black hat hackers. Not only can their personal information be stolen in hack attacks against large targets, but hackers also attack people in a number of ways. The

A big bullseye

Target is investigating a security breach that began the day before Thanksgiving, involving stolen credit and debit card information of millions of its retail customers.

About the retailer

Opened 1962 in Minneapolis

Online E-commerce site launched in 1999

Employees 361,000 worldwide

Gross profit $22.73 billion

Chairman, President, CEO Gregg Steinhafel

Popularity No. 2 discount chain (behind Walmart) in the U.S.

Stores 1,797 in 49 U.S. states; 124 in Canada

Number of stores

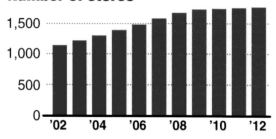

Source: Target Corp., Hoovers, Yahoo Finance
Graphic: Melina Yingling   © 2013 MCT

TARGET

Nov. 27
Criminals gained access to customer information

Dec. 15
Target identified breach, resolved the issue

40 million
Names, credit, debit card numbers, expiration dates, three-digit security codes stolen

Data can be sold on the black market; used to create counterfeit cards

Millions of people had their credit card information exposed after hackers broke into networks belonging to the discount retailer Target in 2013.

World Wide Web offers multiple possible threats from black hat hackers. Typically, individuals become hacking victims when they are tricked into downloading malware or they visit an unsecured website, where a malicious program downloads to their computer.

Hackers essentially set traps for people on the internet. Phishing emails are one common means of hacking private computers and have been around for decades. These messages appear to come from a legitimate source. They appear to come from banks, social networks, or email service providers. Many phishing messages include corporate logos and contact information to make them look real. They seem to inform the recipient of a problem with messages or notifications, or of a need to update account information. A link or an attachment is included, but instead of taking the recipient to the corporate site, it downloads malware onto his or her computer.

There are numerous other ways for malware to load onto a personal computer or device. These programs might be attached to a video or a sound file that has been downloaded from peer-to-peer sharing networks. Drive-by downloads happen when users visit certain websites. A malicious script runs and installs the malware without the user's permission. Pop-up windows that open on some websites may contain viruses or other malware that runs when users click on them. Using social engineering practices, they often look like warnings and urge the users to click on them. Ironically, many disguise themselves as virus protection updates.

Malware programs used by hackers include Trojan Horse viruses, which are bits of code that open a back door onto a user's computer. Key readers are another type of malware. These programs record keystrokes as the user types them, allowing a hacker to figure out login information and passwords. Some malware can completely hijack a computer's functions without the user's knowledge. These so-called "zombie computers" join together to form a "botnet." Botnets are networks of such machines that hackers join together to perform large-scale attacks. A botnet gives hackers the processing power of a super computer, creating a powerful tool that they can use to carry out attacks.

Chapter 4

ATTACK AND COUNTERATTACK

Hacking incidents have become much more common in recent years, and the security breaches have become more serious. It is no longer possible to see a hack of a government agency, a retailer, a social network, or a service as an isolated incident. Some institutions—especially government and military departments—are attacked on an almost daily basis. Other organizations may be hacked once, but the breach is big enough to cause real problems for the people whose data has been compromised. White hat hackers work to make these breaches a thing of the past, even as their black hat opponents try to find new ways to undermine digital security.

HACKER TECHNIQUES

Black hat hackers look for security weak points they can use to break into secure systems. They often use a technique called "social engineering." The first step might be to perform public surveillance. The hackers gather information that might be useful. If planning to hack a company, they might make a list of employees and then build files on each of them, starting with an individual's work email address and following it through to that person's social media profile. They discover personal information, from the employees' addresses to the names of their family members.

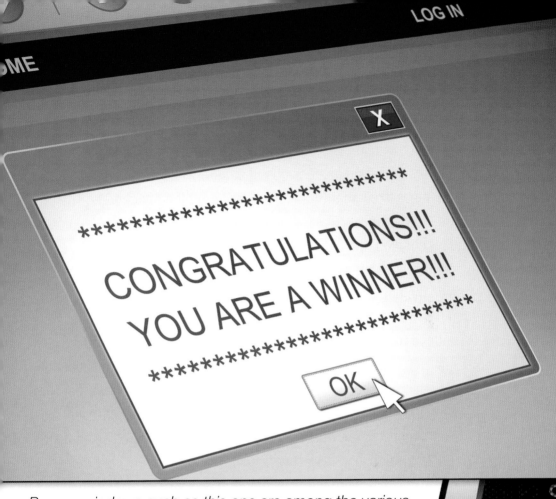

Pop-up windows such as this one are among the various methods hackers use to load malicious software onto the computers of unsuspecting users.

The hackers then study the types of computer systems and software the company uses. They can find this information from several sources, including the marketing materials of software vendors who advertise their clients or by calling the company and pretending to be an employee or vendor.

The hacker puts the gathered knowledge together to gain access. This access may come in the form of phishing. The hacker sends an email to employees that appears to include a harmless attachment. Instead, the attachment opens a malware program that can take over that user's computer. The emails often seem to come from someone in a position of authority within the company, making it more likely that the recipient will trust the attachment. The malware program gives the hacker a backdoor to the user's computer. By using that opening, the hacker may be able to access a network or even the company's entire system.

Once the hackers gain access, they might change mail settings so that any warnings of security breaches are blocked. The hackers continue to work on the computer they breached, loading more malicious software onto it. These may gather passwords or secretly take screenshots and forward them to the hackers. These malware programs are often loaded into the computer's random-access memory, where they are less likely to be discovered by antivirus programs than if they were downloaded onto the hard drive. Other malware may be programmed to arrive as bits of code and then reassemble into a malicious program.

The hackers then move through the system, uncovering more information and gaining increasingly higher levels of access until they are ready to attack. A black hat hacker may spend weeks gathering information, but it might take just a few minutes to use that information to launch an attack that could consist of anything from widespread data theft to shutting systems down.

Hackers use a number of other tricks to cause chaos. They might be able to exploit weak wireless networks to access user computers. Public wireless networks, such as those in libraries and airports, are usually unsecured. Hackers may try to unleash malware on other users of public networks. They may also search these networks for any information left behind by other users.

Denial-of-service attacks often exploit already-hacked computers. Hackers activate malware and use it to bring thousands of computers together to create a botnet. They then bombard a server with requests, often by hitting a website again and again. All of those computers bombarding a website at once crashes the server and it goes down. Although the data is not being compromised, the website's ability to do business is severely affected.

PRYING EYES

Back in the 1980s, a high-profile hack was a major news story. Today, black hat hacking incidents have become much more common. However, they still receive as much attention—or possibly more, because of society's growing reliance on computers. Several significant data breaches have occurred in recent years, affecting the personal information of private citizens and celebrities, as well as bringing corporate secrets to light.

The retail chain Target was hit by hackers in a major incident that took place in 2013. Credit and debit card information belonging to forty million customers was stolen. The hackers accessed the company's system by first attacking a small air conditioning business that worked with Target. The hackers used malware delivered via email to steal the access information of several employees, and then used that data to break into Target's systems.

THE SONY PICTURES HACK

In November 2014, a group of hackers calling themselves the Guardians of Peace used a worm to break into servers at Sony Pictures Entertainment. They released a flood of stolen data that included confidential employee information and private communications. The hackers locked employees out of Sony computers and took control of several Twitter accounts. Malware introduced by the hackers erased data from more than three thousand computers and from more than five hundred servers.

The Guardians of Peace also threatened to commit an act of terrorism unless Sony cancelled the release of a film called *The Interview*, which is a comedy about a plan to assassinate North Korean dictator Kim Jong-un. US intelligence officials later linked the Guardians of Peace to the North Korean government, though North Korea has denied involvement. After the cyber attack, Sony had to put aside $15 million to deal with its aftermath. The company also upgraded its cyber security to prevent any future hacks.

Among the tactics that are being used by some companies to protect data include taking the offense by halting breaches before they happen and looking for unusual log-in patterns. Another strategy is to ensure that all data is encrypted, no matter where it is stored. Companies also want to monitor carefully who has access to data.

Christopher Chaney (center) talks to reporters in 2011. Chaney was one of the individuals charged in connection with the iCloud hacks of 2014.

Celebrities were the victims of a massive hacking incident in 2014. Hackers accessed iCloud accounts and stole private photos belonging to celebrities. The iCloud accounts linked to smartphones and other devices, enabling the hackers to access data that were never meant to be shared. Personal photos of dozens of celebrities were among the stolen images and were later released on the internet. The hack itself was relatively simple and came down to using a software program that tried possible password combinations. Through their actions, the hackers violated the privacy of those people.

The IRS was the victim of a major hacking incident in 2015. Hackers used an IRS website feature that allowed tax filers to see their past tax payments. The hackers apparently used personal details found elsewhere on the internet to answer security questions and access the site. More than seven hundred thousand Social Security numbers were stolen.

FENDING OFF THE HACKERS

Keeping valuable information and personal data out of the hands of hackers is a constant challenge. Tight cyber security is key to protecting data. White hat hackers advise customers to ensure that their software programs are up to date. Out-of-date software might be more susceptible to viruses and hacking.

Limiting employee access to only the computers and systems they need to do their work can also cut down on the risk of a widespread hacking incident. Every point of access given to an employee is a potential gateway for a hacker to use to get deeper into a company's systems. Businesses can help employees defend against breaches by creating a company culture in which employees learn how to spot risks and report them to the IT department. A strong security culture also instructs workers on how to create strong passwords and how to keep them secure by changing them often and how to be careful with email attachments. Instead of automatically clicking on attachments—even those that appear to come from their superiors within the company—employees should ask themselves whether they need to open it if it appears suspicious. They also should hover their mouse over any links to see where

Antivirus software, such as the programs sold by Norton, offer protection against many types of cyber attacks, including malware. Keeping this software current can help defend against hackers.

they lead and to avoid clicking on links that they didn't expect to receive. Keeping track of when files have been opened and whether anything has been added to them can also help head off a potential data breach.

Keeping software updated and antivirus programs current is vital. Weaknesses in older programs are often well known to hackers. Once a program loses online support, it stops receiving updates necessary to prevent new threats. The same is true for antivirus programs. New malware comes along all the time, and older programs may not be able to see it as a threat. Even encryption programs should be updated. Encryption keys make it more difficult for hackers to get into systems, but older encryption certificates can be tricked into allowing access.

White hat hackers sometimes set traps of their own to catch their black hat counterparts. Honeypots are computers or servers that are intentionally left unsecured to tempt black hat hackers. Security personnel can catch the hackers as they break in, or watch them in action to see how they gain access. In this way, they turn the tables on the hackers by using them to discover weaknesses or vulnerabilities so that they can fix those problems.

CHAPTER 5

GATHERING IN THE SHADOWS

Hackers operate in all parts of the world, and the interconnectivity made possible by the World Wide Web allows them to pursue targets from any location. Many hackers join groups that dedicate their energies to one particular interest or target.

GOVERNMENT-SPONSORED HACKING

Cyber warfare refers to the use of government-paid hackers to breach the security of computer networks in other countries to cause damage or steal information. The United States takes the possibilities of cyber warfare very seriously. In 2009, the US Department of Defense created the United States Cyber Command (USCYBERCOM) to unify the military's cyber warfare efforts. The command's mission is to bring together the military's cyberspace resources and expand its ability to carry out and defend against cyber attacks.

Other US agencies have conducted their own cyber warfare efforts. The Equation Group was a network that carried out hacking operations for the National Security Agency. These hackers executed operations in at least forty-two countries, including Iran, China, Russia, Brazil, Mexico, the United Kingdom, and the United States. Possibly thousands of computers have been victimized by the group's malware.

Nir Gaist is an Israeli entrepreneur and cyber security expert. His company, Nyotron, developed the groundbreaking "Paranoid" technology, putting it at the forefront of international cyber warfare.

The United States is also suspected of working with Israel to develop the Stuxnet worm, which was released in 2010. The worm severely damaged Iran's nuclear program by targeting key equipment used to make nuclear material. The worm spread quickly but targeted only specific systems. The Russia-based software security group Kaspersky Lab later noted similarities between Stuxnet and malware linked to the Equation Group, raising the possibility that the group worked with the Stuxnet developers or built the worm itself.

Hacked by LIZARD SQUAD - **OFFICIAL CYBER CAL**

FOLLOW CYBERCALIPHATE ON TV

@LIZARDMAFIA

@UMGROBERT

@UMG_CHRIS

In January 2015, the Lizard Squad hacked a website belonging to Malaysia Airlines and defaced it with this picture of a well-dressed reptile.

Many other nations also engage in cyber warfare. Germany's military set up its Computer Network Operations unit in 2006 to carry out cyber attacks, although it wasn't activated until 2012. In war-torn Syria, the Syrian Electronic Army was developed to implement hacking attacks against enemies of the government of President Bashar al-Assad. The group has launched attacks against the US government and media organizations, sometimes managing to steal passwords and deface websites. Bureau 121 is North Korea's secretive cyber-warfare agency. The organization is believed to be behind the Sony Pictures hack.

Black hat hackers other than cyber-warfare organizations sometimes pool their resources to go after their targets. One black hat group called Hacking Team operates as a company out of Italy. This group sells malware to other hackers, including governments. Ironically, Hacking Team was hacked in 2015. Data including its employees and customers was released online. Hacking Team's clients included US agencies such as the FBI and several repressive governments, including Saudi Arabia and Vietnam.

HACKTIVISM

Not every ideologically driven hacker works for a government. Some of these hackers are sometimes called "hacktivists" because they are hacking in an attempt to bring attention to some cause or to damage an organization that they believe causes harm. Their activity might range from simply defacing a website to serious data breaches or dedicated denial-of-service attacks. Hacktivists often have good intentions, and in some cases their hacks have brought important issues to light. However, the fact that they access servers and networks without permission makes their activities illegal. In the hacking world, they are usually seen as black hats or gray hats. The global collective Anonymous is possibly the best-known hacktivist group. Its members have pursued targets ranging from the online payment company PayPal to terrorist organizations such as the Islamic State of Iraq and the Levant.

A group called the Lizard Squad carried out a series of distributed denial-of-service attacks against gaming sites, at times shutting down the Sony PlayStation Network and Microsoft Xbox Live. The Impact Team hacked the controversial dating website Ashley Madison in 2015, stealing the personal data of its thirty-seven million users. They used algorithms to crack user passwords and access accounts. When the site's operators didn't respond to demands to close the site, the Impact Team released stolen data that included names, addresses, and credit card information.

THE FACES OF HACKING

A number of hackers have become famous—or infamous—for their exploits. Among white hat hackers, Apple cofounder Steve Wozniak stands out. Before joining with Steve Jobs to form Apple, Inc., Wozniak was a phone phreaker and hacker with a deep interest in how communication technology worked. He was expelled from the University of Colorado–Boulder for hacking into the school's computer system. His knowledge played a key role in Apple's early successes, as he was responsible for designing the hardware, circuit board, and operating systems for the company's first computers.

Tim Berners-Lee, the British computer scientist who invented the World Wide Web, also hacked communications systems. Berners-Lee was a tinkerer from a very early age who once built his own computer from spare parts, some of which he salvaged from the trash. He worked as an engineer with several telecommunications companies before he took a job at the European Organization for Nuclear Research (CERN), which led to creating the web.

WikiLeaks founder Julian Assange hacked a number of targets as a teenager. Working under the handle "Mendax," he cracked into US Department of Defense facilities, Citibank, Motorola, and other high-profile companies and organizations. In 1991, he was arrested for hacking into the Australian branch of the Canadian

Well-known hacker Kevin Mitnick is legally barred from using a computer. He had to get permission to use one while writing his book The Art of Deception.

telecommunications firm Nortel and convicted—although he did not receive jail time, in part, because he did not show any malicious intent.

Kevin Mitnick was one of the most famous early hackers. Mitnick began hacking in 1979, when he was sixteen years old. In 1988, he was convicted of illegally accessing the computer system of the Digital Equipment Corporation and copying software. He was sentenced to a year in jail and three years of court supervision. However, he fled before the supervision period was over and became a fugitive. Mitnick was caught with hacking equipment after more than two years on the run and sentenced to five years in prison. After his release, he started a computer company. On the other side of the law, the computer security expert and physicist Tsutomu Simomura played a key role in helping the FBI capture Mitnick.

GATHERING HACKERS

Hackers tend to form communities, exchanging techniques and ideas with one another through message boards. White hat and gray hat hackers gather for annual conferences. The Black Hat Briefings bring together hackers and representatives from companies and government agencies to talk about security concerns. These events started informally in 1997 but have since grown into significant industry events. Briefings take place regularly in cities such as Las Vegas, Nevada; Barcelona, Spain; Amsterdam, the Netherlands; and Abu Dhabi, United Arab Emirates. Special briefings dedicated to US government agencies take place in Washington, DC. Workshops called

Black Hat Trainings are offered by a number of security vendors, enabling professionals to catch up with new developments in the field and earn professional certifications.

DEF CON is another well-known meeting of hackers. DEF CON started in Las Vegas in 1993 and has grown into one of the world's largest hacker gatherings. Security professionals, government officials, journalists, law enforcement agents, and researchers attend the annual event. Apart from lectures on security and hacking, DEF CON includes competitions and off-beat activities, such as lock-picking and sprawling games of Capture the Flag. Even these low-tech activities can teach security professionals new ways of thinking about how hackers try to get past barriers.

GLOSSARY

algorithm A step-by-step set of rules for solving a problem, especially in mathematics or computing.

bug An error or flaw in a computer's software or hardware that causes a program to fail.

cyberspace The realm of computer networks where electronic communication takes place.

encryption The act of putting data into a coded form.

espionage The act of spying.

exploit To use to one's own advantage.

firewall The sum of security measures intended to prevent unauthorized access to a networked computer.

hacker A person who uses personal computers to break into computer systems.

hacktivism The act of hacking a network or site to promote a cause.

ideology The principles and beliefs that guide an individual or a group.

legitimate Allowed by the law or correct according to the law.

mainframe A large and powerful computer system, often shared by many users.

malicious Intentionally harmful.

malware Software designed to harm or take over a computer, electronic device, or network.

manipulate To manage or influence skillfully, especially in an unfair manner.

network A system of interconnected computers and other devices through which information is shared.

phishing The act of using electronic communications to trick people into giving up personal information.

server A computer or program that supplies data or resources to other machines on a network.

social engineering The act of tricking people into revealing information.

virus A segment of code planted illegally and designed to copy itself while shutting down computers, networks, and servers.

worm A program planted illegally that damages files and programs on a computer or system.

FOR MORE INFORMATION

Computer History Museum
1401 North Shoreline Boulevard
Mountain View, CA 94043
(650) 810-1010
Website: http://www.computerhistory.org
The mission of the Computer History Museum is to preserve and present
for posterity the artifacts and stories of the information age.

Electronic Frontier Foundation
454 Shotwell Street
San Francisco, CA 94110
(415) 436-9333
Website: http://www.eff.org
The Electronic Frontier Foundation is a group with the goal of supporting
internet freedom.

Hacker Highschool
Website: http://www.hackerhighschool.org
Hacker Highschool provides online, downloadable lessons on hacking, cyber
security, and using the internet safely, written specifically for teens.

Internet Society
1775 Wiehle Avenue, Suite 201
Reston, VA 20190-5108

(703) 439-2120

Website: http://www.internetsociety.org

This organization works to address issues relating to the internet, including internet education, standards, and policy.

Media Awareness Network

1500 Merivale Road, 3rd Floor

Ottawa, ON K2E 6Z5

Canada

(613) 224-7721

Website: http://www.media-awareness.ca/english/index.cfm

The website for this Canadian network contains a selection of digital literacy resources for students, teachers, and parents.

WEBSITES

Because of the changing nature of internet links, Rosen Publishing has developed an online list of websites related to the subject of this book. This site is updated regularly. Please use this link to access the list:

http://www.rosenlinks.com/CCMCB/white

FOR FURTHER READING

Allen, John. *Online Privacy and Hacking*. San Diego, CA: ReferencePoint Press, 2014.

Curley, Robert, ed. *Architects of the Information Age* (Computing and Connecting in the 21st Century). New York, NY: Britannica Educational Publishing, 2012.

Curley, Robert. *Computing: From the Abacus to the iPad* (Computing and Connecting in the 21st Century). New York, NY: Britannica Educational Publishing, 2012.

Espejo, Roman. *Policing the Internet*. Detroit, MI: Greenhaven Press, 2012.

Haerens, Margaret. *Hacking and Hackers*. Detroit, MI: Greenhaven Press, 2013.

Mara, Wil. *Software Development: Science, Technology, Engineering*. New York, NY: Children's Press, 2016.

Netzley, Patricia D. *How Serious a Problem Is Computer Hacking?* (In Controversy). San Diego, CA: ReferencePoint Press, 2013.

Parks, Peggy. *Cyberwarfare*. San Diego, CA: ReferencePoint Press, 2012.

Smith, Jonathan. *White Hat Hacking* (High-Tech Jobs). New York, NY: Cavendish Square Publishing, 2015.

Yomtov, Nelson. *Internet Security: From Concept to Consumer*. New York, NY: Children's Press, 2016.

BIBLIOGRAPHY

Boorstin, Julia. "The Sony Hack: One Year Later." CNBC.com, November 24, 2015. (http://www.cnbc.com/2015/11/24/the-sony-hack-one-year -later.html).

Burningham, Grant. "How a White Hat Hacker Breaks Into a Business." *Newsweek,* March 19, 2016. (http://www.wired.com/2015/07 /hackers-remotely-kill-jeep-highway).

Engebretson, Pat. *The Basics of Hacking and Penetration Testing.* Waltham, MA: Syngress, 2011.

Goodin, Dan. "How 'Omnipotent' Hackers Tied to NSA Hid for 14 Years— and Were Found at Last." *Ars Technica*, February 16, 2015. (http:// arstechnica.com/security/2015/02/how-omnipotent-hackers-tied -to-the-nsa-hid-for-14-years-and-were-found-at-last).

Greenberg, Andy. "Hackers Remotely Kill a Jeep on the Highway—With Me in It." *Wired*, July 21, 2015. (https://www.wired.com/2015/07 /hackers-remotely-kill-jeep-highway).

Holmes, David. "What Keeps White Hat Hackers from Turning to the Dark Side?" *Network World*, February 16, 2016. (http://www.networkworld .com/article/3035594/security/what-keeps-white-hat-hackers-from -turning-to-the-dark-side.html).

Leyden, John. "The 30-Year-Old Prank That Became the First Computer Virus." *The Register*, December 14, 2012. (http://www.theregister .co.uk/2012/12/14/first_virus_elk_cloner_creator_interviewed).

Lu, Donna. "When Ethical Hacking Can't Compete." *Atlantic*, December 8, 2015. (http://www.theatlantic.com/technology/archive/2015/12 /white-hat-ethical-hacking-cybersecurity/419355).

Mello, John P., Jr. "Hot Hacker Targets in 2016: Fantasy Sports, Professional Services." *Tech News World*, December 15, 2015. (http://www.technewsworld.com/story/82876.html).

Oriyano, Sean-Philip. *CEHv8: Certified Ethical Hacker Study Guide Version 8 Study Guide*. Indianapolis, IN: Sybex, 2014.

Reuters. "2 W. Germans Get Suspended Sentences as Computer Spies." *Los Angeles Times*, February 16, 1990. (http://articles.latimes.com/1990-02-16/news/mn-667_1_computer-wizards).

Singer, P. W., and Allan Friedman. *Cybersecurity and Cyberwar: What Everyone Needs to Know*. New York, NY: Oxford University Press, 2014.

Vryronis, Panayotis. "Explaining Public Key Cryptography to Non-Geeks." Medium.com, August 27, 2013. (http://articles.latimes.com/1990-02-16/news/mn-667_1_computer-wizards).

Yagoda, Ben. "A Short History of Hack." *New Yorker*, March 6, 2014. (http://www.newyorker.com/tech/elements/a-short-history-of-hack).

Zetter, Kim. "An Unprecedented Look at Stuxnet, the World's First Digital Weapon." *Wired*, November 3, 2014. (http://www.wired.com/2014/11/countdown-to-zero-day-stuxnet).

INDEX

ABOUT THE AUTHOR

Jason Porterfield is a writer and journalist living in Chicago, Illinois. He writes about tech subjects for several publications. Some of his technology books include *Julian Assange and WikiLeaks*, *Tim Berners-Lee*, *Careers as a Cyberterrorism Expert*, and *Conducting Basic and Advanced Searches*.

PHOTO CREDITS